RUBANK

OLO AND ENSEMBLE SERIES

Hasse Suite

Johann Adolph Hasse

Compiled & Edited by Wm. Gower

for TROMBONE

with piano accompaniment

RUBANK®

HAL•LEONARD®

Hasse Suite
Trombone and Piano

•

JOHANN ADOLPH HASSE
Compiled and Edited by Wm. Gower

I — Passepied*

*Passepied = păs-pĭ-ā.

Hasse Suite

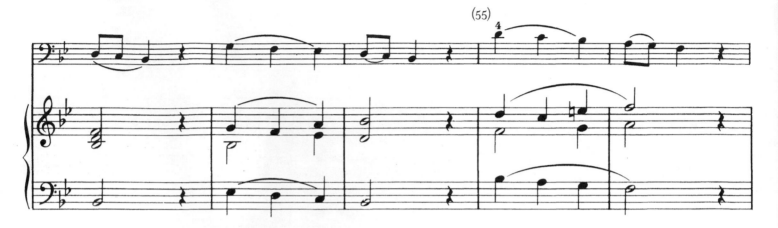

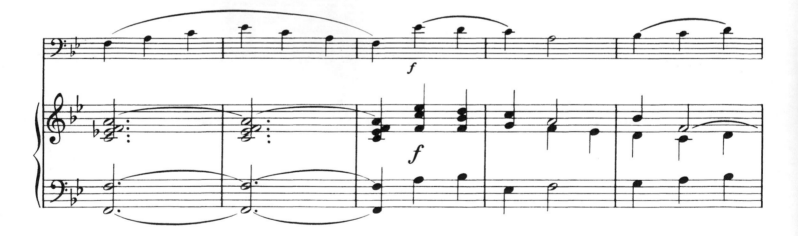

Hasse Suite

II — Arietta

Hasse Suite

Hasse Suite

Hasse Suite

for Trombone with Piano Accompaniment

✱

Johann Adolph Hasse

Compiled and Edited by Wm. Gower

HAL•LEONARD® CORPORATION

7777 W. BLUEMOUND RD. P.O. BOX 13819 MILWAUKEE, WI 53213

Hasse Suite
Trombone and Piano

JOHANN ADOLPH HASSE
(1699-1783)
Compiled and Edited by Wm. Gower

Trombone

•

I — Passepied*

Allegro moderato (♩ = 120)

* Passepied = păs-pĭ-ā.

II—Arietta

III — March

Trombone

III — March

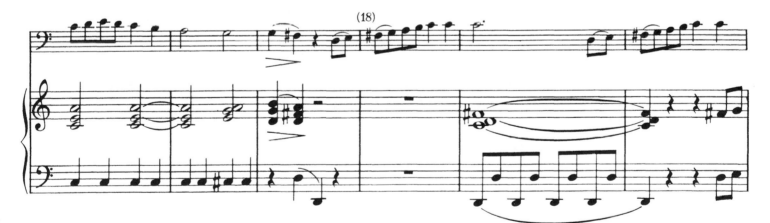

Hasse Suite

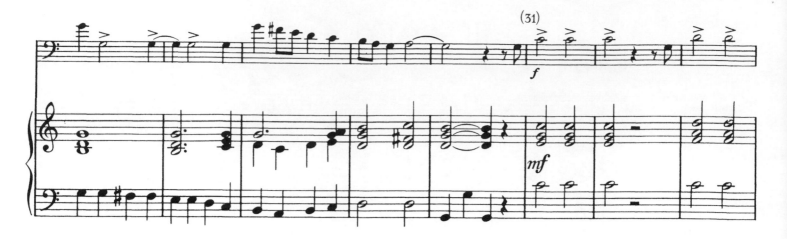

Hasse Suite

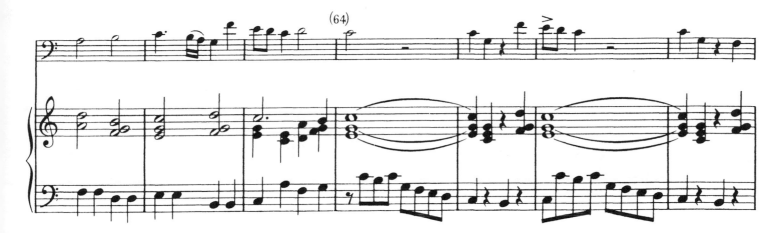

Hasse Suite